Just Be Yourself

Gabi Johnson

BookLeaf Publishing

Presentation by *BookLeaf Publishing*

Web: www.bookleafpub.com

E-mail: info@bookleafpub.com

ISBN: 9789357744188

First edition 2023

DEDICATION

I dedicate this book to myself. Despite all the spiraling, the self-doubt, the distraction, and the fear, you created it. Congratulations on finally publishing something that has been long overdue.

ACKNOWLEDGEMENT

-Thank you to Bookleaf for inspiring me to create this project.

-Thank you Mom for always believing in my dreams to be a writer.

scissorhands

i was confident as a kindergartener.
i made friends easily,
and i was smart and creative.

there was a basket of pencils in DW-4.
one was specifically designated for me.
everyone wanted a turn to use it.

however, there were no special scissors.

my sunshine began to set the day
the rest of my class walked away
while i worked on my project

i sat alone in the library
cutting, cutting, cutting
well, at least trying to

my scissors didn't work
but they didn't listen

i'd come to find out that day
that most people wouldn't.

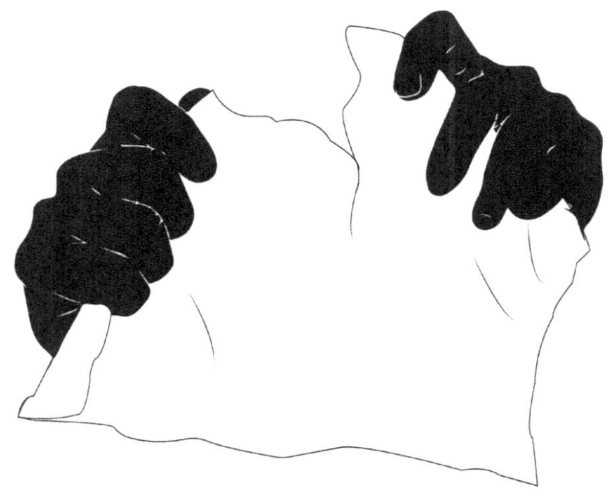

born yesterday

if i was born yesterday…
…it would just be a school
…it would just be a sport
…it would just be a band
…it would just be a book
…it would just be a movie
…it would just be a video game
…it would just be a hairstyle
…it would just be a sequence of numbers
…it would just be an article of clothing
…it would just be a piece of jewelry
…it would just be a picture
…they would just be words.
if i was born yesterday, there would be no racing
hearts,
no clenched throats, no dissociating, no yelling,
no tears.
no fear.
no anger.
no pain.
no helplessness.
no loneliness.
if i was born yesterday, everything would just
be.
nothing more, nothing less.

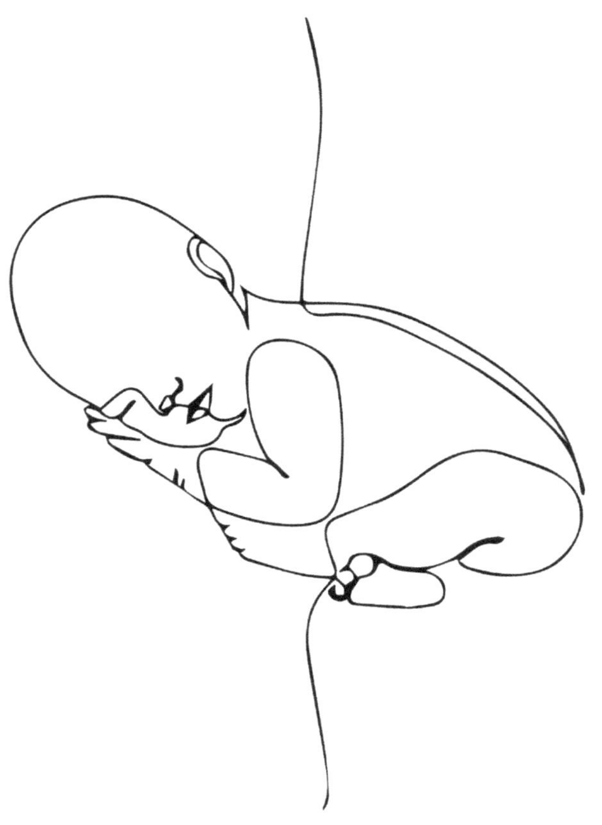

first love

trust me, i didn't want to let you go
you were the one gem nobody had to help me
find;
the one nobody forced me to keep.
you were what made me the most myself.
you felt the most like home in a world with few
safe corners.
you made me feel warm and fuzzy and excited
and joyful
i stopped myself from spending too much time
with you
because i feared this feeling would come to an
end
and it did, it always did.
because nobody ever understood.
the pain of having you a part of my life
the high highs, the low lows
the crying, the longing, the waiting, the hoping
that someday i could share my joy with someone
else
was like hoping someday i'd see a fish fly
so i had to let you go
because feeling lukewarm joy and being able to
share it

will always be better than true joy that must be
kept to myself.

the silk on the mountain

the high i get from being on its peak
makes me feel like i'm on top of the world
i feel heaven brushing against my head
but the peak is a slippery slope
and i'm never able to keep my balance
something or someone always makes me trip
rocks fall, i fall, we roll off into the velvet
underground

a lot of people, their lives were saved by rock n'
roll
but it damn near killed me

armor

i always thought my anger was my armor
and that rage was my shield
and sometimes they were
but they usually only made more people attack
me
dropping my defenses is always scary
when i feel an attack coming and i don't react
i drop all my armor and expose myself
i feel cold, i feel naked, i feel vulnerable.
but my lack of armor makes them let me be
and then, i feel invincible.

the feelings bottle

the bottle of my emotions
is clear at the top then slowly fades
to a solid black at the bottom
the emotions closest to the top
are most visible
easiest to release from it &
the easiest to understand
the ones at the bottom
they're the ones hidden the best
and have the hardest time escaping
because if they ever did my entire life would
take a change for the worse
so they shall never see light

addiction

i was so addicted to ugliness
i'd find a flaw in anything with beauty.

i was so addicted to lacking
it never felt right to be receiving.

i was so addicted to struggling
that i couldn't allow myself to thrive.

i was so addicted to storms
that on sunny days i'd find a way to
create my own.

i was so addicted to pain
that i didn't know what to do without it.

hear me

i walk in a world where
i feel i am never heard
yet i can see, there are
1,103 monthly listeners
227,455 monthly listeners
457,536 monthly listeners
482,845 monthly listeners
2,011,940 monthly listeners
10,383,170 monthly listeners

there's someone else
who can hear me
there has to be.

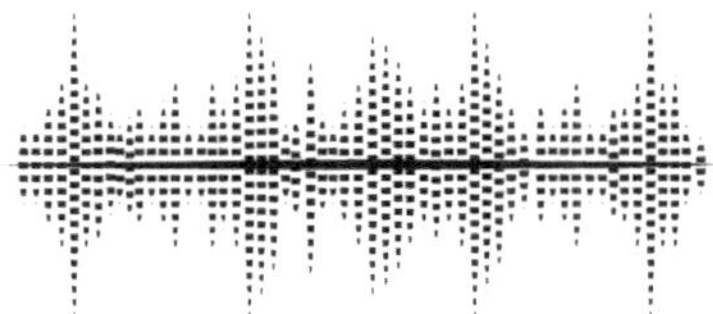

ode to the daredevils

this is an ode to the ones who stood their ground
in a world full of naysayers
here's to the ones who couldn't make their
collars blue
or their schedule 9-5
here's to the ones who keep their heads up when
their friends
are buying homes and driving benzes
while they don't know if they can sell enough art
to make rent this month

here's to the ones who blocked out the noise,
"art is useless"
"you need to be a productive member of
society"
"you can't really expect to make a living from
that?"
here's to the ones who never had a "plan b"
here's to the ones who knew doing anything
with their lives besides what they loved was not
an option,
no matter what other people had to say about it.
i wish i was as brave as you.

pick me

even when everything is smooth
i find somewhere to pick
i know it's unproductive
i know it causes problems
i know it makes things worse
and next thing i know i'm bleeding
crying
yelling at you
because "you hurt me"
and you just walk away as i realize
i am the one who keeps hurting me.

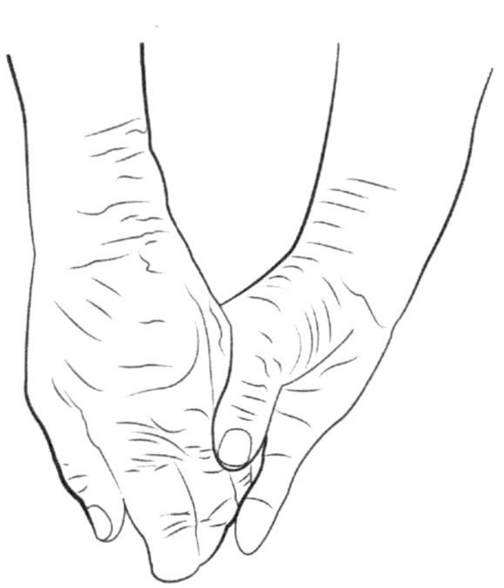

just be yourself

you will never remember my middle name,
my birthday,
my major in college,
my favorite artists,
even though i'll always remember yours.

you will never be able to meet my needs
or understand my boundaries
or reassure me enough.

you will never use the correct "their"
you will never call me pet names
you will never put the toilet seat down
you'll never drive with a seatbelt on
you will never add vegetables to your meals

i expected too much from you,
and I've accepted that i cannot change you.
you cannot validate me.
and it's taken me all these years to realize
that is okay.
just be yourself.

there will never be a right time

there will never be a right time
"i'll do it when i get that new job"
and then you do, and you use your
car breaking down as an excuse not to

"i'll do it after i fix my car"
and then you do, and you use your
pet getting sick as an excuse not to

"i'll do it after my pet gets better"
and then they do, and you use your
malaise with your body as an excuse not to

"i'll do it once i lose weight"
and then you lose it, and you use your life
just being plain old imperfect
as an excuse not to

"i'll do it when my life gets better"
and then it never completely fits
your definition of better.

and before you know it,
you've lost your chance.

words will save me from you

i like to think that one day
words will save me from
the 4 AM nausea on a monday morning
as the cold rain hits the window

the 7 AM dread
as i try to hold onto my slumber

barely eating enough breakfast
because sleep is more important

walking into the fake laughs, the fake smiles
hiding my constant discomfort

the urge to just walk away
during the middle of the day

the urge to run away
and start a new life

the end of the day
which brings a false sense of relief

the sunset beaming against my car
the rays in my eyes making my drive difficult

the headaches above my neck
as i pull into the driveway

my leg pain
my foot pain
my back pain
my heart pain

my questioning
as to how everyone else does this
without feeling like they're dying

wondering why
i always go straight home

my feeling of
"i should be doing something else"
and never having time for that
"something else" because
i am so drained

one day the very thing that ruined me
will be the thing that brings me
out of the trenches

rocky road

words don't roll off my back
they tumble like pebbles, stones
and settle into carbuncles

around my neck
across my shoulders
down my spine

carrying it all
feels like carrying
the weight of the world sometimes

i shiver with disgust writing this
wishing i didn't always
have to curl up in a ball as i sleep

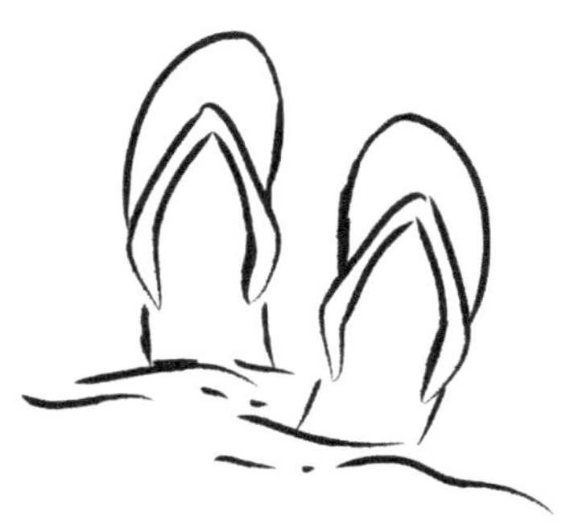

the chatter

"it's your fault you don't have friends!

maybe you should've
played sports as a kid
instead of playing a violin

maybe you should have been
friends with the girl
who tried to cut your hair in class
instead of the girls people laughed at

maybe you should have changed
the station that aired your favorite music
you know people like you
aren't supposed to like stuff like that

maybe you shouldn't have
listened to your parents
been more reckless and
started drinking at 14

maybe you should have
worn more clothes
that made you feel uncomfortable
like an impostor

maybe you should have
chose a different school
and stopped running away
from what society wants you to be

maybe you should take
our advice for once, don't you see
we're trying to protect you!

maybe if you weren't YOU
you wouldn't have such a
hard time in this world which is clearly
just the way it OUGHT TO BE and you,
you are the stain on its beauty"

the fog

i'm sorry it always seems like
i'm somewhere else
the fog follows me wherever i go
and sucks me away
constantly trying to find a place
that feels safer to me

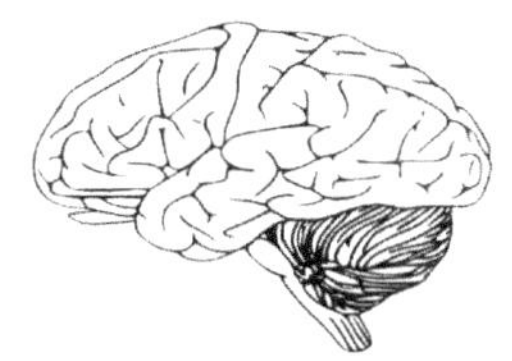

growing pains

looking back
my adolescent pain
seems so silly
but i'm never
too quick to laugh
because i still see the scars
every single day.

old jeans

i've been wearing you since i was sixteen
the skinniest of skinny jeans
buy 1, get 1
from american eagle.
i walked in you during my first boyfriend,
my first break up.
friends who came and friends who gone
through me trying to hold on
but slipping away to no avail
you watched me fail,
and you watched me grow.
i put you on today and fell into my old ways
i know so much more now
all the bad people are gone
all the bad places i never have to go back to
the nasty, fuzzy blue denim
is suffocating my legs
they
don't
fit
i'm not the same person anymore
so why do i still act this way?